THE PSAI

&

THE ODES OF SOLOMON

FROM THE SERIES

THE FORGOTTEN BOOKS OF EDEN

EDITED BY

RUTHERFORD H. PLATT, JR.
[1926]

RESURRECTED BY

ABELA PUBLISHING, LONDON
[2013]

THE FORGOTTEN BOOKS OF EDEN

THE PSALMS OF SOLOMON
&
THE ODES OF SOLOMON

Abela Publishing,
London
United Kingdom
2013

ISBN-13: 978-1-909302-30-3

email Books@AbelaPublishing.com

www.AbelaPublishing.com/solomon.html

THE JUDGMENT OF SOLOMON

Henri-Frederic Schopin

[1804 - 1880]

ACKNOWLEDGEMENTS

The Publisher acknowledges the work that

RUTHERFORD H. PLATT, JR.

did in editing this unique volume

in a time well before any electronic media was in use.

* * * * * * *

33% of the publisher's profit

from the sale from this book

will be donated to charities.

* * * * * * *

YESTERDAY'S BOOKS

Raising funds for

TODAY'S CHARITIES

CONTENTS

THE PSALMS OF SOLOMON

INTRODUCTION

THIS collection of eighteen war songs are the gift of an ancient Semitic writer. The original manuscript has perished but fortunately Greek translations have been preserved, and recently a Syriac version of the same songs has turned up and was published in English for the first time in 1909 by Dr. Rendel Harris.

The date of the writing may be established at the middle of the First Century B. C. because the theme of these songs is that of Pompey's actions in Palestine and his death in Egypt in 48 B. C. These psalms had an important position and were widely circulated in the early Church. They are frequently referred to in the various Codexes and histories of the first few centuries of the Christian Era.

Later, they became lost through inexplicable reasons; and have only been recovered for our use after the lapse of many centuries. Besides the literary value of the trumpet-like rhythm of these verses, we have here a chapter of stirring ancient history written by an eyewitness. Pompey comes out of the West. He uses battering-rams on the fortifications. His soldiers defile the altar.

He is slain in Egypt after a fearful career. In the "righteous" of these psalms we see the Pharisees; in the "sinners" we see the Sadducees. It is an epic of a great people in the throes of a great crisis.

I

"They became insolent in their prosperity . . . ."

I cried unto the Lord when I was in distress,
Unto God when sinners assailed.
Suddenly the alarm of war was heard before me;
I said, He will hearken to me for I am full of righteousness.
I thought in my heart that I was full of righteousness,
Because I was well off and had become rich in children.
Their wealth spread to the whole earth,
And their glory unto the end of the earth.
They were exalted unto the stars;
They said they would never fan.
But they became insolent in their prosperity,
And they were without understanding,
Their sins were in secret,
And even I had no knowledge of them.
Their transgressions went beyond those of the heathen before them;
They utterly polluted the holy things of the Lord.

II

The desecration of Jerusalem; captivity, murder, and raping. A psalm of utter despair.

When the sinner waxed proud, with a battering-ram he cast down fortified walls,
And thou didst not restrain him.
Alien nations ascended Thine altar,
They trampled it proudly with their sandals;
Because the sons of Jerusalem had defiled the holy things of the Lord,
Had profaned with iniquities the offerings of God.
Therefore He said: Cast them far from Me;

. . . . . .

It was set at naught before God,
It was utterly dishonoured;
The sons and the daughters were m grievous captivity,
Sealed was their neck, branded was it among the nations.
According to their sins hath He done unto them,
For He hath left them in the hands of them that prevailed.
He hath turned away His face from pitying them,
Young and old and their children together;
For they had done evil one and all, in not hearkening.
And the heavens were angry,
And the earth abhorred them;
For no man upon it had done what they did,
And the earth recognized all
Thy righteous judgements, O God.
They set the sons of Jerusalem to be mocked at in return for the harlots in her;
Every wayfarer entered in in the full light of day.

They made mock with their transgressions, as they themselves were wont to do;
In the full light of day they revealed their iniquities.
And the daughters of Jerusalem were defiled in accordance with Thy judgement,
Because they had defiled themselves with unnatural intercourse.
I am pained in my bowels and my inward parts for these things.
And yet I will justify Thee, O God, in uprightness of heart,
For in Thy judgements is Thy righteousness displayed, O God.
For Thou hast rendered to the sinners according to their deeds,
Yea, according to their sins, which were very wicked.
Thou hast uncovered their sins, that Thy judgement might be manifest;
Thou hast wiped out their memorial from the earth.
God is a righteous judge,
And he is no respecter of persons.
For the nations reproached Jerusalem, trampling it down;
Her beauty was dragged down from the throne of glory.
She girded on sackcloth instead of comely raiment,
A rope was about her head instead of a crown.
She put off the glorious diadem which God had set upon her,
In dishonour was her beauty cast upon the ground.
And I saw and entreated the Lord and said,
Long enough, O Lord has Thine hand been heavy on Israel, in bringing the nations upon them.
For they have made sport unsparingly in wrath and fierce anger;
And they will make an utter end, unless Thou, O Lord, rebuke them in Thy wrath.
For they have done. it not in zeal, but in lust of soul,
Pouring out their wrath upon us with a view to rapine.
Delay not, O God, to recompense them on their heads,
To turn the pride of the dragon into dishonour.

And I had not long to wait before God showed me the insolent one
 Slain on the mountains of Egypt,
 Esteemed of less account than the least, on land and sea;
His body, too, borne hither and thither on the billows with much insolence,
 With none to bury him, because He had rejected him with dishonour.
He reflected not that he was man,
 And reflected not on the latter end;
He said: I will be lord of land and sea;
 And he recognized not that it is God who is great,
 Mighty in His great strength.
He is king over the heavens,
 And judgeth kings and kingdoms.
It is He who setteth me up in glory,
 And bringeth down the proud to eternal destruction in dishonour,
 Because they knew Him not.
And now behold, ye princes of the earth, the judgement of the Lord,
 For a great king and righteous is He, judging all that is under heaven.
Bless God, ye that fear the Lord with wisdom,
 For the mercy of the Lord will ~e upon them that fear Him, m the Judgement;
So that He will distinguish between the righteous and the sinner,
 And recompense the sinners for ever according to their deeds;
And have mercy on the righteous, delivering him from the affliction of the sinner,
 And recompensing the sinner for what he bath done to the righteous.

For the Lord is good to them that call upon Him in patience,
Doing according to His mercy to His pious ones,
Establishing them at all times before Him in strength.
Blessed be the Lord for ever before His servants.

III

Righteousness versus Sin.

Why sleepest thou, O my soul,
 And blessest not the Lord?
Sing a new song,
 Unto God who is worthy to be praised.
Sing and be wakeful against His awaking,
 For good is a psalm sung to God from a glad heart.
The righteous remember the Lord at all times,
 With thanksgiving and declaration of the righteousness of the Lord's judgements.
The righteous despiseth not the chastening of the Lord;
 His will is always before the Lord.
The righteous stumbleth and holdeth the Lord righteous:
 He falleth and looketh out for what God will do to him;
He seeketh out whence his deliverance will come.
 The steadfastness of the righteous is from God, their deliverer;
There lodgeth not in the house of the righteous sin upon sin.
 The righteous continually searcheth his house,
To remove utterly all iniquity done by him in error.
 He maketh atonement for sins of ignorance by fasting and afflicting his soul,
And the Lord counteth guiltless every pious man and his house.
 The sinner stumbleth and curseth his life
The day when he was begotten, and his mother's travail.
 He addeth sins to sins, while he liveth;
He falleth--verily grievous is his fall--and riseth no more.
 The destruction of the sinner is forever,
And he shall not be remembered, when the righteous is visited.
 This is the portion of sinners forever.

But they that fear the Lord shall rise to life eternal,
And their life shall be in the light of the Lord, and shall come to an end no more.

IV

A conversation of Solomon with the Men-pleasers.

Wherefore sittest thou, O profane man, in the council of the pious,
Seeing that thy heart is far removed from the Lord,
Provoking with transgressions the God of Israel?
Extravagant in speech, extravagant in outward seeming beyond all men,
Is he that is severe of speech in condemning sinners in judgement.
And his hand is first upon him as though he acted in zeal,
And yet he is himself guilty in respect of manifold sins and of wantonness.
His eyes are upon every woman without distinction;
His tongue lieth when he maketh contract with an oath.
By night and in secret he sinneth as though unseen,
With his eyes he talketh to every woman of evil compacts.
He is swift to enter every house with cheerfulness as though guileless.
Let God remove those that live in hypocrisy in the company of the pious,
Even the life of such an one with corruption of his flesh and penury.
Let God reveal the deeds of the men-pleasers,
The deeds of such an one with laughter and derision;
That the pious may count righteous the judgement of their God,
When sinners are removed from before the righteous,
Even the man-pleaser who uttereth law guilefully.
And their eyes are fixed upon any man's house that is still secure,
That they may, like the Serpent, destroy the wisdom of . . . with words of transgressors,
His words are deceitful that he may accomplish his wicked desire.

He never ceaseth from scattering families as though they were orphans,
Yea, he layeth waste a house on account of his lawless desire.
He deceiveth with words, saying, There is none that seeth, or judgeth.
He fills one house with lawlessness,
And then his eyes are fixed upon the next house,
To destroy it with words that give wing to desire.
Yet with all these his soul like Sheol, is not sated.
Let his portion, O Lord, be dishonoured before thee;
Let him go forth groaning, and come home cursed.
Let his life be spent in anguish, and penury, and want, O Lord; Let his sleep be beset with pains and his awaking with perplexities.
Let sleep be withdrawn from his eyelids at night;
Let him fail dishonourably in every work of his hands.
Let him come home empty-handed to his house,
And his house be void of everything wherewith he could sate his appetite.
Let his old age be spent in childless loneliness until his removal by death.
Let the flesh of the men-pleasers be rent by wild beasts,
And let the bones of the lawless lie dishonoured in the sight of the sun.
Let ravens peck out the eyes of the hypocrites.
For they have laid waste many houses of men, in dishonour,
And scattered them in their lust;
And they have not remembered God,
Nor feared God in all these things;
But they have provoked God's anger and vexed Him.
May He remove them from off the earth,
Because with deceit they beguiled the souls of the flawless.

Blessed are they that fear the Lord in their flawlessness;
 The Lord shall deliver them from guileful men and sinners,
 And deliver us from every stumbling-block of the lawless (men).
Let God destroy them that insolently work all unrighteousness,
 For a great and mighty judge is the Lord our God in
righteousness.
Let Thy mercy, O Lord, be upon all them that love Thee.

V

A statement of the philosophy of the indestructibility of matter. One of the tenets of modern physics.

O Lord God, I will praise Thy name with joy,
In the midst of them that know Thy righteous judgements.
For Thou art good and merciful, the refuge of the poor;
When I cry to Thee, do not silently disregard me.
For no man taketh spoil from a mighty man;
Who, then, can take aught of a that Thou hast made, except Thou Thyself givest?
For man and his portion lie before Thee in the balance;
He cannot add to, so as to enlarge, what has been prescribed by Thee.
O God, when we are in distress we call upon Thee for help,
And Thou dost not turn back our petition, for Thou art our God.
Cause not Thy hand to be heavy upon us,
Lest through necessity we sin.
Even though Thou restore us not, we will not keep away;
But unto Thee will we come.
For if I hunger, unto Thee will I cry, O God;
And *Thou* wilt give to me.
Birds and fish dost Thou nourish,
In that Thou givest rain to the steppes that green grass may spring up,
So to prepare fodder in the steppe for every living thing;
And if they hunger, unto Thee do they lift up their face.
Kings and rulers and peoples *Thou* dost nourish, O God;
And who is the help of the poor and needy, if not Thou, O Lord?
And Thou wilt hearken--for who is good and gentle but thou?--
Making glad the soul of the humble by opening Thine hand in mercy.

Man's goodness is bestowed grudgingly and ...;
 And if he repeat it without murmuring, even that is marvellous.
But Thy gift is great in goodness and wealth,
 And he whose hope is set on Thee shall have no lack of gifts.
Upon the whole earth is Thy mercy, O Lord, in goodness.
Happy is he whom God remembereth in granting to him a due sufficiency;
 If a man abound overmuch, he sinneth.
Sufficient are moderate means with righteousness,
 And hereby the blessing of the Lord becomes abundance with righteousness.
They that fear the Lord rejoice in good gifts,
 And thy goodness is upon Israel in Thy kingdom.
Blessed is the glory of the Lord, for He is our king.

VI

A song of hope and fearlessness and peace.

Happy is the man whose heart is fixed to call upon the name of the Lord;
When he remembereth the name of the Lord, he will be saved.
His ways are made even by the Lord,
And the works of his hands are preserved by the Lord his God.
At what he sees in his bad dreams, his soul shall not be troubled;
When he passes through rivers and the tossing of the seas, he shall not be dismayed.
He ariseth from his sleep, and blesseth the name of the Lord:
When his heart is at peace, he singeth to the name of his God,
And he entreateth the Lord for all his house.
And the Lord heareth the prayer of every one that feareth God,
And every request of the soul that hopes for Him doth the Lord accomplish.
Blessed is the Lord, who showeth mercy to those who love Him in sincerity.

VII

The fine old doctrine--"Thou art our Shield!"

Make not Thy dwelling afar from us, O God;
 Lest they assail us that hate us without cause.
For Thou hast rejected them, O God;
 Let not their foot trample upon Thy holy inheritance.
Chasten us Thyself in Thy good pleasure;
 But give us not up to the nations;
For, if Thou sendest pestilence,
 Thou Thyself givest it charge concerning us;
For Thou art merciful,
 And wilt not be angry to the point of consuming us.

While Thy name dwelleth in our midst, we shall find mercy;
 And the nations shall not prevail against us.
For Thou art our shield,
 And when we call upon Thee, Thou hearkenest to us;
For Thou wilt pity the seed of Israel for ever
 And Thou wilt not reject them:
But we shall, be under Thy yoke for ever,
 And under the rod of Thy chastening.
Thou wilt establish us in the time that Thou helpest us,
 Showing mercy to the house of Jacob on the day wherein Thou didst promise to help them.

VIII

Some remarkable similes of war creeping on Jerusalem. A survey of the sins that brought all this trouble.

Distress and the sound of war hath my ear heard,
The sound of a trumpet announcing slaughter and calamity,
The sound of much people as of an exceeding high wind,
As a tempest with mighty fire sweeping through the Negeb.
And I said in my heart, Surely God judgeth us;
A sound I hear moving towards Jerusalem, the holy city
My loins were broken at what I heard, my knees tottered;
My heart was afraid, my bones were dismayed like flax.
I said: They establish their ways in righteousness.

I thought upon the judgments of God since the creation of heaven and earth;
I held God righteous in His judgements which have been from of old.
God bare their sins in the full light of day;
All the earth came to know the righteous judgements of God.
In secret places underground their iniquities were committed to provoke Him to anger;
They wrought confusion, son with mother and father with daughter;
They committed adultery, every man with his neighhour's wife.
They concluded covenants with one another with an oath touching these things;
They plundered the sanctuary of God, as though there was no avenger.
They trode the altar of the Lord, coming straight from all manner of uncleanness;
And with menstrual blood they defiled the sacrifices, as though

these were common flesh.
They left no sin undone, wherein they surpassed not the heathen.

Therefore God mingled for them a spirit of wandering;
And gave them to drink a cup of undiluted wine, that they might become drunken.
He brought him that is from the end of the earth, that smiteth mightily;
He decreed war against Jerusalem, and against her land.
The princes of the land went to meet him with joy: they said unto him:
Blessed be thy way! Come ye, enter ye in with peace.
They made the rough ways even, before his entering in;
They opened the gates to Jerusalem, they crowned its walls.

As a father entereth the house of his sons, so he entered Jerusalem in peace;
He established his feet there in great safety.
He captured her fortresses and the wall of Jerusalem;
For God Himself led him in safety, while they wandered.
He destroyed their princes and every one wise in counsel;
He poured out the blood of the inhabitants of Jerusalem, like the water of uncleanness.
He led away their sons and daughters, whom they had begotten in defilement.

They did according to their uncleanness, even as their fathers had done:
They defiled Jerusalem and the things that had been hallowed to the name of God.
But God hath shown Himself righteous in His judgements upon the nations of the earth;

And the pious servants of God are like innocent lambs in their midst.
Worthy to be praised is the Lord that judgeth the whole earth in His righteousness.

Behold, now, O God, Thou hast shown us Thy judgement in Thy righteousness;
Our eyes have seen Thy judgements, O God.
We have justified Thy name that is honoured for ever;
For Thou are the God of righteousness, judging Israel with chastening.

Turn, O God, Thy mercy upon us, and have pity upon us;
Gather together the dispersed of Israel, with mercy and goodness;
For Thy faithfulness is with us,

And though we have stiffened our neck, yet Thou art our chastener;
Overlook us not, O our God, lest the nations swallow us up, as though there were none to deliver.

But Thou art our God from the beginning,
And upon Thee is our hope set, O Lord;
And we will not depart from Thee,
For good are Thy judgements upon us.
Ours and our children's be Thy good pleasure for ever;
O Lord, our Saviour, we shall never more be moved.
The Lord is worthy to be praised for His judgements with the mouth of His pious ones;
And blessed be Israel of the Lord for ever.

IX

The exile of the tribes of Israel. A reference to the covenant which God made with Adam. (See the First Book of Adam and Eve, Chap. III, Verse 7).

When Israel was led away captive into a strange land,
When they fell away from the Lord who redeemed them,
They were cast away from the inheritance, which the Lord had given them.
Among every nation were the dispersed of Israel according to the word of God,
That Thou mightest be justified, O God, in Thy righteousness by reason of our transgressions:
For Thou art a just judge over all the peoples of the earth.
For from Thy knowledge none that doeth unjustly is hidden,
And the righteous deeds of Thy pious ones are before Thee, O Lord;
Where, then, can a man hide himself from Thy knowledge, O God?
Our works are subject to our own choice and power
To do right or wrong in the works of our hands;
And in Thy righteousness Thou visitest the sons of men.
He that doeth righteousness layeth up life for himself with the Lord;
And he that doeth wrongly forfeits his life to destruction;
For the judgements of the Lord are given in righteousness to every man and his house.
Unto whom art Thou good, O God, except to them that call upon the Lord?
He cleanseth from sins a soul when it maketh confession, when it maketh acknowledgement;

For shame is upon us and u on our faces on account of all these things.
And to whom doth He forgive sins, except to them that have sinned?
Thou blessest the righteous, and dost not reprove them for the sins that they have committed;
And Thy goodness is upon them that sin, when they repent.
And, now, Thou art our God, and we the people whom Thou hast loved:
Behold and show pity, O God of Israel, for we are Thine;
And remove not Thy mercy from us, lest they assail us.
For Thou didst choose the seed of Abraham before all the nations,
And didst set Thy name upon us, O Lord,
And Thou wilt not reject us for ever.
Thou madest a covenant with our fathers concerning us;
And we hope in Thee, when our soul turneth unto Thee.
The mercy of the Lord be upon the house of Israel for ever and ever.

X

A glorious hymn. Further reference to the eternal covenant between God and Man.

Happy is the man whom the Lord remembereth with reproving,
And whom He restraineth from the way of evil with strokes
That he may be cleansed from sin, that it may not be multiplied.
He that maketh ready his back for strokes shall be cleansed,
For the Lord is good to them that endure chastening.
For He maketh straight the ways of the righteous,
And doth not pervert them by His chastening.
And the mercy of the Lord is upon them that love Him in truth,
And the Lord remembereth His servants in mercy.
For the testimony is in the law of the eternal covenant,
The testimony of the Lord is on the ways of men in His visitation.
Just and kind is our Lord in His judgements for ever,
And Israel shall praise the name of the Lord in gladness.
And the pious shall give thanks in the assembly of the people;
And on the poor shall God have mercy in the gladness of Israel;
For good and merciful is God for ever,
And the assemblies of Israel shall glorify the name of the Lord.
The salvation of the Lord be upon the house of Israel unto everlasting gladness!

XI

Jerusalem hears a trumpet and stands on tiptoe to see her children returning from the North, East and West.

Blow ye in Zion on the trumpet to summon the saints,
Cause ye to be heard in Jerusalem the voice of him that bringeth good tidings;
For God hath had pity on Israel in visiting them.
Stand on the height, O Jerusalem, and behold thy children,
From the East and the West, gathered together by the Lord;
From the North they come in the gladness of their God,
From the isles afar off God hath gathered them.
High mountains hath He abased into a plain for them;
The hills fled at their entrance.
The woods gave them shelter as they passed by;
Every sweet-smelling tree God caused to spring up for them,
That Israel might pass by in the visitation of the glory of their God.
Put on, O Jerusalem, thy glorious garments;
Make ready thy holy robe;
For God hath spoken good concerning Israel, for ever and ever.
Let the Lord do what He hath spoken concerning Israel and Jerusalem;
Let the Lord raise up Israel by His glorious name.
The mercy of the Lord be upon Israel for ever and ever.

XII

An appeal for family tranquility and peace and quiet at home.

O Lord, deliver my soul from the lawless and wicked man,
From the tongue that is lawless and slanderous, and speaketh lies and deceit.
Manifoldly twisted are the words of the tongue of the wicked man,
Even as among a people a fire that burneth up their beauty.
So he delights to fill houses with a lying tongue,
To cut down the trees of gladness which setteth on fire transgressors,
To involve households in warfare by means of slanderous lips.

May God remove far from the innocent the lips of transgressors by bringing them to want
And may the bones of slanderers be scattered far away from them that fear the Lord!
In flaming fire perish the slanderous tongue far away from the pious!
May the Lord preserve the quiet soul that hateth the unrighteous;
And may the Lord establish the man that followeth peace at home.

The salvation of the Lord be upon Israel His servant for ever;
And let the sinners perish together at the presence of the Lord;
But let the Lord's pious ones inherit the promises of the Lord.

XIII

Of Solomon. A Psalm. Comfort for the righteous.

The right hand of the Lord hath covered me;
The right hand of the Lord hath spared us.
The arm of the Lord hath saved us from the sword that passed through,
From famine and the death of sinners.
Noisome beasts ran upon them:
With their teeth they tore their flesh,
And with their molars crushed their bones.
But from all these things the Lord delivered us.
The righteous was troubled on account of his errors,
Lest he should be taken away along with the sinners;
For terrible is the overthrow of the sinner;
But not one of all these things toucheth the righteous.
For not alike are the chastening of the righteous for sins done in ignorance,
And the overthrow of the sinners.
Secretly is the righteous chastened,
Lest the sinner rejoice over the righteous.
For He correcteth the righteous as a beloved son.
And his chastisement is as that of a first-born.
For the Lord spareth His pious ones,
And blotteth out their errors by His chastening.
For the life of the righteous shall be for ever;
But sinners shall be taken away into destruction,,
And their memorial shall be found no more.
But upon the pious is the mercy of the Lord,
And upon them that fear Him His mercy.

XIV

Sinners "love the brief day spent in companionship with their sin." Profound wisdom, beautifully expressed.

Faithful is the Lord to them that love Him in truth,
To them that endure His chastening,
To them that walk in the righteousness of His commandments,
In the law which He commanded us that we might live.
The pious of the Lord shall live by it for ever;
The Paradise of the Lord, the trees of life, are His pious ones.
Their planting is rooted for ever;
They shall not be plucked up all the days of heaven:
For the portion and the inheritance of God is Israel.
But not so are the sinners and transgressors,
Who love the brief day spent in companionship with their sin;
Their delight is in fleeting corruption,
And they remember not God.
For the ways of men are known before Him at all times,
And He knoweth the secrets of the heart before they come to pass.
Therefore their inheritance is Sheol and darkness and destruction
And they shall not be found in the day when the righteous obtain mercy;
But the pious of the Lord shall inherit life in gladness.

XV

The psalmist restates the great philosophy of Right and Wrong.

When I was in distress I called upon the name of the Lord,
 I hoped for the help of the God of Jacob and was saved;
 For the hope and refuge of the poor art Thou, O God.
For who, O God, is strong except to give thanks unto Thee in truth?
 And wherein is a man powerful except in giving thanks to Thy name?
A new psalm with song in gladness of heart,
 The fruit of the lips with the well-tuned instrument of the tongue,
 The first fruits of the lips from a pious and righteous heart--
He that offereth these things shall never be shaken by evil;
 The flame of fire and the wrath against the unrighteous shall not touch him,
When it goeth forth from the face of the Lord against sinners,
 To destroy all the substance of sinners,
For the mark of God is upon the righteous that they may be saved.
Famine and sword and pestilence shall be far from the righteous,
 For they shall flee away from the pious as men pursued in war;

But they shall pursue sinners and overtake them,
  And they that do lawlessness shall not escape the judgement of God;
As by enemies experienced in war shall they be overtaken,
  For the mark of destruction is upon their forehead.
And the inheritance of sinners is destruction and darkness,
  And their iniquities shall pursue them unto Sheol beneath.
Their inheritance shall not be found of their children,
  For sins shall lay waste the houses of sinners.
And sinners shall perish for ever in the day of the Lord's judgement,
  When God visiteth the earth with His judgement.
But they that fear the Lord shall find mercy therein,
  And shall live by the compassion of their God;
But sinners shall perish for ever.

XVI

The psalmist again expresses profound truth--"For if Thou givest not strength, who can endure chastisement?"

When my soul slumbered being afar from the Lord, I had all but slipped down to the pit,
When I was far from God, my soul had been well-nigh poured out unto death,
I had been nigh unto the gates of Sheol with the sinner,
When my soul departed from the Lord God of Israel--
Had not the Lord helped me with His everlasting mercy.

He pricked me, as a horse is pricked, that I might serve Him,
My saviour and helper at all times saved me.
I will give thanks unto Thee, O God, for Thou hast helped me to my salvation;
And hast not counted me with sinners to my destruction.
Remove not Thy mercy from me, O God,
Nor Thy memorial from my heart until I die.
Rule me, O God, keeping me back from wicked sin,
And from every wicked woman that causeth the simple to stumble.
And let not the beauty of a lawless woman beguile me,
Nor any one that is subject to unprofitable sin.

Establish the works of my hands before Thee,
And preserve my goings in the remembrance of Thee.
Protect my tongue and my lips with words of truth;

Anger and unreasoning wrath put far from me.
Murmuring, and impatience in affliction, remove far from me
When, if I sin, Thou chastenest me that I may return unto Thee.
But with goodwill and cheerfulness support my soul;
When Thou strengthenest my soul, what is given to me will be sufficient for me.
For if *Thou* givest not strength,
Who can endure chastisement with poverty?
When a man is rebuked by means of his corruption,
Thy testing of him is in his flesh and in the affliction of poverty.
If the righteous endureth in all these trials, he shall receive mercy from the Lord.

XVII

"They set a worldly monarchy . . . . they lay waste the Throne of David!' A poetic narrative about the utter disintegration of a great nation.

O Lord, Thou art our King for ever and ever,
For in Thee, O God, doth our soul glory.
How long are the days of man's life upon the earth?
As are his days, so is the hope set upon him.
But *we* hope in God, our deliverer;
For the might of our God is for ever with mercy,
And the kingdom of our God is for ever over the nations in judgement.

Thou, O Lord, didst choose David to be king over Israel,
And swaredst to him touching his seed that never should his kingdom fail before Thee.
But, for our sins, sinners rose up against us;
They assailed us and thrust us out;
What Thou hadst not promised to them, they took away from us with violence.
They in no wise glorified Thy honourable name;
They set a worldly monarchy in place of that which was their excellency;
They laid waste the throne of David in tumultuous arrogance.
But Thou, O God, didst cast them down, and remove their seed from the earth,

In that there rose up against them a man that was alien to our race.
According to their sins didst Thou recompense them, O God;
So that it befell them according to their deeds.
God showed them no pity;
He sought out their seed and let not one of them go free.
Faithful is the Lord in all His judgements
Which He doeth upon the earth.

The lawless one laid waste our land so that none inhabited it,
They destroyed young and old and their children together.
In the heat of His anger He sent them away even unto the west,
And He exposed the rulers of the land unsparingly to derision.
Being an alien the enemy acted proudly,
And his heart was alien from Our God.
And all things whatsoever he did in Jerusalem,
As also the nations in the cities to their gods.

And the children of the covenant in the midst of the mingled peoples surpassed them in evil.
There was not among them one that wrought in the midst of Jerusalem mercy and truth.
They that loved the synagogues of the pious fled from them,
As sparrows that fly from their nest.
They wandered in deserts that their lives might be saved

from harm,

And precious in the eyes of them that lived abroad was any that escaped alive from them.

Over the whole earth were they scattered by lawless men.

For the heavens withheld the rain from dropping upon the earth,

Springs were stopped that sprang perennially out of the deeps, that ran down from lofty mountains.

For there was none among them that wrought righteousness and justice;

From the chief of them to the least of them all were sinful;

The king was a transgressor, and the judge disobedient, and the people sinful.

Behold, O Lord, and raise up unto them their king, the son of David,

At the time in the which Thou seest, O God, that he may reign over Israel Thy servant.

And gird him with strength, that he may shatter unrighteous rulers,

And that he may purge Jerusalem from nations that trample her down to destruction.

Wisely, righteously he shall thrust out sinners from the inheritance,

He shall destroy the pride of the sinner as a potter's vessel.

With a rod of iron he shall break in pieces all their substance,

He shall destroy the godless nations with the word of his mouth;

At his rebuke nations shall flee before him,

And he shall reprove sinners for the thoughts of their heart.

And he shall gather together a holy people, whom he shall lead in righteousness,
And he shall judge the tribes of the people that has been sanctified by the Lord his God.
And he shall not suffer unrighteousness to lodge any more in their midst,
Nor shall there dwell with them any man that knoweth wickedness,
For he shall know them, that they are all sons of their God.
And he shall divide them according to their tribes upon the land,
And neither sojourner nor alien shall sojourn with them any more.
He shall judge peoples and nations in the wisdom of his righteousness. *Selah.*

And he shall have the heathen nations to serve him under his yoke;
And he shall glorify the Lord in a place to be seen of all the earth;
And he shall purge Jerusalem, making it holy as of old:
So that nations shall come from the ends of the earth to see his glory,
Bringing as gifts her sons who had fainted.
And to see the glory of the Lord, wherewith God hath glorified her.
And he shall be a righteous king, taught of God, over them,
And there shall be no unrighteousness in his days in their midst,

For all shall be holy and their king the anointed of the Lord.
For he shall not put his trust in horse and rider and bow,
Nor shall he multiply for himself gold and silver for war,
Nor shall he gather confidence from a multitude for the day of battle.
The Lord Himself is his king, the hope of him that is mighty through his hope in God.

All nations shall be in fear before him,
For he will smite the earth with the word of his mouth for ever.
He will bless the people of the Lord with wisdom and gladness,
And he himself will be pure from sin, so that he may rule a great people.
He will rebuke rulers, and remove sinners by the might of his word;
And relying upon his God, throughout his days he will not stumble;
For God will make him mighty by means of His holy spirit,
And wise by means of the spirit of understanding, with strength and righteousness.
And the blessing of the Lord will be with him: he will be strong and stumble not;
His hope will be in the Lord: who then can prevail against him?
He will, be mighty in his works, and strong in the fear of God,
He will be shepherding the flock of the Lord faithfully and

righteously,
And will suffer none among them to stumble in their pasture.
He will lead them all aright,
And there will be no pride among them that any among them should be oppressed.
This will be the majesty of the king of Israel whom God knoweth;
He will raise him up over the house of Israel to correct him.
His words shall be more refined than costly gold, the choicest;
In the assemblies he will judge the peoples, the tribes of the sanctified.
His words shall be like the words of the holy ones in the midst of sanctified peoples.
Blessed be they that shall be in those days,
In that they shall see the good fortune of Israel which God shall bring to pass in the gathering together of the tribes.
May the Lord hasten His mercy upon Israel!
May He deliver us from the uncleanness of unholy enemies!
The Lord Himself is our king for ever and ever.

XVIII

With this psalm end the warlike Songs of Solomon.

Lord, Thy mercy is over the works of Thy hands for ever;
Thy goodness is over Israel with a rich gift.
Thine eyes look upon them, so that none of them suffers want;
Thine ears listen to the hopeful prayer of the poor.
Thy judgements are executed upon the whole earth in mercy;
And Thy love is toward the seed of Abraham, the children of Israel.
Thy chastisement is upon us as upon a first-born, only-begotten son,
To turn back the obedient soul from folly that is wrought in ignorance.
May God cleanse Israel against the day of mercy and blessing,
Against the day of choice when
Blessed shall they be that shall be in those days,
He bringeth back His anointed.
In that they shall see the goodness of the Lord which He shall perform for the generation that is to come,
Under the rod of chastening of the Lord's anointed in the fear of his God,
In the spirit of wisdom and righteousness and strength;
That he may direct every man in the works of righteousness by the fear of God,

That he may establish them all before the Lord,
A good generation living in the fear of God in the days of mercy. Selah.

Great is our God and glorious, dwelling in the highest.
It is He who hath established in their courses the lights of heaven for determining seasons from year to year,
And they have not turned aside from the way which He appointed them.
In the fear of God they pursue their path every day,
From the day God created them and for evermore.
And they have erred not since the day He created them.
Since the generations of old they have not withdrawn from their path,
Unless God commanded them so to do by the command of His servants.

THE ODES OF SOLOMON

INTRODUCTION

HERE are some of the most beautiful songs of peace and joy that the world possesses. Yet their origin, the date of their writing, and the exact meaning of many of the verses remain one of the great literary mysteries.

They have come down to us in a single and very ancient document in Syriac language. Evidently that document is a translation from the original Greek. Critical debate has raged around these Odes; one of the most plausible explanations is that they are songs of newly baptized Christians of the First Century.

They are strangely lacking in historical allusions. Their radiance is no reflection of other days. They do not borrow from either the Old Testament or the Gospels. The inspiration of these verses is first-hand. They remind you of Aristides' remark, "*A new people with whom something Divine is mingled.*" Here is vigor and insight to which we can find parallels only in the most exalted parts of the Scriptures.

For these dazzling mystery odes, we owe our translation to J. Rendel Harris, MA., Hon. Fellow of Clare College, Cambridge. He says about them: "There does not seem to be anything about which everyone seem agreed unless it be that the Odes are of singular beauty and high spiritual value."

ODE 1

1 The Lord is on my head like a crown, and I shall not be without Him.
2 They wove for me a crown of truth, and it caused thy branches to bud in me.
3 For it is not like a withered crown which buddeth not: but thou livest upon my head, and thou hast blossomed upon my head.
4 Thy fruits are full-grown and perfect, they are full of thy salvation.

ODE 2

(No part of this Ode has ever been identified.)

ODE 3

The first words of this Ode have disappeared.

1 . . . I put on:
2 And his members are with him. And on them do I stand, and He loves me:
3 For I should not have known how to love the Lord, if He had not loved me.
4 For who is able to distinguish love, except the one that is loved?
5 I love the Beloved, and my soul loves Him:
6 And where His rest is, there also am I;
7 And I shall be no stranger, for with the Lord Most High and Merciful there is no grudging.
8 I have been united to I-run, for the Lover has found the Beloved,
9 And because I shall love Him that, is the Son, I shall become a son;
10 For he that is joined to Him that is immortal, will also himself become immortal;
11 And he who has pleasure in the Living One, will become living.
12 This is the Spirit of the Lord, which doth not lie, which teacheth the sons of men to know His ways.
13 Be wise and understanding and vigilant. Hallelujah.

ODE 4

This Ode is important because of the historical allusion with which it commences. This may refer to the closing of the temple at Leontopolis in Egypt which would date this writing about 73 A. D.

1 No man, O my God, changeth thy holy place;
2 And it is not (possible) that he should change it and put it
in another place: because he hath no power over it:
3 For thy sanctuary thou hast designed before thou didst
make (other) places:
4 That which is the older shall not be altered by those that
are younger than itself.
5 Thou has given thy heart, O Lord, to thy believers: never
wilt thou fail, nor be without fruits:
6 For one hour of thy Faith is more precious than all days
and years.
7 For who is there that shall put on thy grace, and be hurt?
8 For thy seal is known: and thy creatures know it: and thy
(heavenly) hosts possess it: and the elect archangels are clad
with it.
9 Thou hast given us thy fellowship: it was not that thou
wast in need of us: but that we are in need of thee:
10 Distill thy dews upon us and open thy rich fountains that
pour forth to us milk and honey:
11 For there is no repentance with thee that thou shouldest
repent of anything that thou hast promised:
12 And the end was revealed before thee: for what thou

gavest, thou gavest freely:
13 So that thou mayest, not draw them back and take them again:
14 For all was revealed before thee as God, and ordered from the beginning before thee: and thou, O God, hast made all things. Hallelujah.

ODE 5

This Ode has strangely appeared in a speech by Salome in another ancient work called the Pistis Sophia.

1 I will give thanks unto thee, O Lord, because I love thee;
2 O Most High, thou wilt not forsake me, for thou art my hope:
3 Freely I have received thy grace, I shall live thereby:
4 My persecutors will come and not see me:
5 A cloud of darkness shall fall on their eyes; and an air of thick gloom shall darken them:
6 And they shall have no light to see: they may not take hold upon me.
7 Let their counsel become thick darkness, and what I have cunningly devised, let it return upon their own heads:
8 For they have devised a counsel, and it did not succeed:
9 For my hope is upon the Lord, and I will not fear, and because the Lord is my salvation, I will not fear:
10 And He is as a garland on my head and I shall not be moved; even if everything should be shaken, I stand firm;
11 And if all things visible should perish, I shall not die; because the Lord is with me and I am with Him. Hallelujah.

ODE 6

First century universalism is revealed in an interesting way in verse 10.

1 As the hand moves over the harp, and the strings speak.
2 So speaks in my members the Spirit of the Lord, and I
speak by His love.
3 For it destroys what is foreign, and everything that is
bitter:
4 For thus it was from the beginning and will be to the end,
that nothing should be His adversary, and nothing should
stand up against Him.
5 The Lord has multiplied the knowledge of Himself, and is
zealous that these things should be known, which by His
grace have been given to us.
6 And the praise of His name He gave us: our spirits praise
His holy Spirit.
7 For there went forth a stream and became a river great and
broad;
8 For it flooded and broke up everything and it brought
(water) to the Temple:
9 And the restrainers of the children of men were not able to
restrain it, nor the arts of those whose business it is to
restrain waters;
10 For it spread over the face of the whole earth, and filled
everything: and all the thirsty upon earth were given to
drink of it;
11 And thirst was relieved and quenched: for from the Most

High the draught was given.
12 Blessed then are the ministers of that draught who are entrusted with that water of His:
13 They have assuaged the dry lips, and the will that had fainted they have raised up;
14 And souls that were near departing they have caught back from death:
15 And limbs that had fallen they straightened and set up:
16 They gave strength for their feebleness and light to their eyes:
17 For everyone knew them in the Lord, and they lived by the water of life for ever. Hallelujah.

ODE 7

A wonderfully, simple and joyful psalm on the Incarnation.

1 As the impulse of anger against evil, so is the impulse of joy over what is lovely, and brings in of its fruits without restraint:
2 My joy is the Lord and my impulse is toward Him: this path of mine is excellent:
3 For I have a helper, the Lord.
4 He hath caused me to know Himself, without grudging, by His simplicity: His kindness has humbled His greatness.
5 He became like me, in order that I might receive Him:
6 He was reckoned like myself in order that I might put Him on;
7 And I trembled not when I saw Him: because He was gracious to me:
8 Like my nature He became that I might learn Him and like my form, that I might not turn back from Him:
9 The Father of knowledge is the word of knowledge:
10 He who created wisdom is wiser than His works:
11 And He who created me when yet I was not knew what I should do when I came into being:
12 Wherefore He pitied me in His abundant grace: and granted me to ask from Him and to receive from His sacrifice:
13 Because He it is that is incorrupt, the fulness of the ages and the Father of them.

14 He hath given Him to be seen of them that are His, in
order that they may recognize Him that made them: and
that they might not suppose that they came of themselves:
15 For knowledge He hath appointed as its way, He hath
widened it and extended it; and brought to all perfection;
16 And set over it the traces of His light, and I walked
therein from the beginning even to the end.
17 For by Him it was wrought, and He was resting in the
Son, and for its salvation He will take hold of everything;
18 And the Most High shall be known in His Saints, to
announce to those that have songs of the coming of the
Lord;
19 That they may go forth to meet Him, and may sing to
Him with joy and with the harp of many tones:
20 The seers shall come before Him and they shall be seen
before Him,
21 And they shall praise the Lord for His love: because He is
near and beholdeth.
22 And hatred shall be taken from the earth, and along with
jealousy it shall be drowned:
23 For ignorance hath been destroyed, because the
knowledge of the Lord hath arrived.
24 They who make songs shall sing the grace of the Lord
Most High;
25 And they shall bring their songs, and their heart shall be
like the day: and like the excellent beauty of the Lord their
pleasant song:

26 And there shall neither be anything that breathes without knowledge, nor any that is dumb:
27 For He hath given a mouth to His creation, to open the voice of the mouth towards Him, to praise Him:
28 Confess ye His power, and show forth His grace.
Hallelujah.

ODE 8

Note the sudden transition from the person of the Psalmist to the person of the Lord (v. 10). This is like the canonical Psalter in style.

1 Open ye, open ye your hearts to the exultation of the Lord:
2 And let your love be multiplied from the heart and even to the lips,
3 To bring forth fruit to the Lord [fruit], holy [fruit], and to talk with watchfulness in His light.
4 Rise up, and stand erect, ye who sometime were brought low:
5 Tell forth ye who were in silence, that your mouth hath been opened.
6 Ye, therefore, that were despised, be henceforth lifted up, because your righteousness hath been exalted.
7 For the right hand of the Lord is with you: and He is your helper:
8 And peace was prepared for you, before ever your war was.
9 Hear the word of truth, and receive the knowledge of the Most High.
10 Your flesh has not known what I am saying to you neither have your hearts known what I am showing to you.
11 Keep my secret, ye who are kept by it:
12 Keep my faith, ye who are kept by it.
13 And understand my knowledge, ye who know me in truth.

14 Love me with affection, ye who love:
15 For I do not turn away my face from them that are mine;
16 For I know them, and before they came into being I took
knowledge of them, and on their faces I set my seal:
17 I fashioned their members: my own breasts I prepared for
them, that they might drink my holy milk and live thereby.
181 took pleasure in them and am not ashamed of them:
19 For my workmanship are they and the strength of my
thoughts:
20 Who then shall rise up against my handiwork, or who is
there that is not subject to them?
21 I willed and fashioned mind and heart: and they are
mine, and by my own right hand I set my elect ones:
22 And my righteousness goeth before them and they shall
not be deprived of my name, for it is with them.
23 Ask, and abound and abide in the love of the Lord,
24 And yet beloved ones in the Beloved: those who are kept,
in I Iim that liveth:
25 And they that are saved in Him that was saved;
26 And ye shall be found incorrupt in all ages to the name of
your Father. Hallelujah.

ODE 9

We shall never know surely whether the wars referred to here are spiritual or actual outward wars.

1 Open your ears and I will speak to you. Give me your souls that I may also give you my soul,
2 The word of the Lord and His good pleasures, the holy thought which He has devised concerning his Messiah.
3 For in the will of the Lord is your salvation, and His thought is everlasting life; and your end is immortality.
q Be enriched in God the Father, and receive the thought of the Most High.
5 Be strong and be redeemed by His grace.
6 For I announce to you peace, to you His saints;
7 That none of those who hear may fall in war, and that those again who have known Him may not perish, and that those who receive may not be ashamed.
8 An everlasting crown for ever is Truth. Blessed are they who set it on their heads:
9 A stone of great price is it; and there have been wars on account of the crown.
10 And righteousness hath taken it and hath given it to you.
11 Put on the crown in the true covenant of the Lord.
12 And all those who have conquered shall be written in His book.
13 For their book is victory which is yours. And she (Victory) sees you before her and wills that you shall be saved. Hallelujah.

ODE 10

A vigorous little Ode in which Christ Himself is the speaker.

1 The Lord hath directed my mouth by His word: and He
hath opened my heart by His light: and He hath caused to
dwell in me His deathless life;
2 And gave me that I might speak the fruit of His peace:
3 To convert the souls of them who are willing to come to
Him; and to lead captive a good captivity for freedom.
4 I was strengthened and made mighty and took the world
captive;
5 And it became to me for the praise of the Most High, and
of God my Father.
6 And the Gentiles were gathered together who were
scattered abroad.
7 And I was unpolluted by my love for them, because they
confessed me in high places: and the traces of the light were
set upon their heart:
8 And they walked in my life and were saved and became
my people for ever and ever. Hallelujah.

ODE 11

A beautiful sketch of Paradise regained and the blessedness of those who have returned to the privileges of the fallen Adam.

1 My heart was cloven and its flower appeared; and grace sprang up in it: and it brought forth fruit to the Lord,
2 For the Most High clave my heart by His Holy Spirit and searched my affection towards Him: and filled me with His love.
3 And His opening of me became my salvation; and I ran in His way in His peace, even in the way of truth:
4 From the beginning and even to the end I acquired His knowledge:
5 And I was established upon the rock of truth, where He had set me up:
6 And speaking waters touched my lips from the fountain of the Lord plenteously:
7 And I drank and was inebriated with the living water that doth not die;
8 And my inebriation was not one without knowledge, but I forsook vanity and turned to the Most High my God,
9 And I was enriched by His bounty, and I forsook the folly which is diffused over the earth; and I stripped it off and cast it from me:
10 And the Lord renewed me in His raiment, and possessed me by His light, and from above He gave me rest in incorruption;

11 And I became like the land which blossoms and rejoices
in its fruits:
12 And the Lord was like the sun shining on the face of the
land;
13 He lightened my eyes, and my face received the dew; and
my nostrils enjoyed the pleasant odour of the Lord;
14 And He carried me to His Paradise; where is the
abundance of the pleasure of the Lord;
15 And I worshipped the Lord on account of His glory; and I
said, Blessed, O Lord, are they who are planted in thy land!
and those who have a place in thy Paradise;
16 And they grow by the fruits of the trees. And they have
changed from darkness to light.
17 Behold! all thy servants are fair, who do good works, and
turn away from wickedness to the pleasantness that is thine:
18 And they have turned back the bitterness of the trees
from them, when they were planted in thy, land;
19 And everything became like a relic of thyself, and
memorial for ever of thy faithful works.
20 For there is abundant room in thy Paradise, and nothing
is useless therein;
21 But everything is filled with fruit; glory be to thee, O God,
the delight of Paradise for ever. Hallelujah.

ODE 12

An exceptionally high level of spiritual thought.

1 He hath filled me with words of truth; that I may speak the
same;
2 And like the flow of waters flows truth from my mouth,
and my lips show forth His fruit.
3 And He has caused His knowledge to abound in me,
because the mouth of the Lord is the true Word, and the
door of His light;
4 And the Most High hath given it to His words, which are
the interpreters of His own beauty, and the repeaters of His
praise, and the confessors of His counsel, and the heralds of
His thought, and the chasteners of His servants.
5 For the swiftness of the Word is inexpressible, and like its
expression is its swiftness and force;
6 And its course knows no limit. Never doth it fail, but it
stands sure, and it knows not descent nor the way of it.
7 For as its work is, so is its end: for it is light and the
dawning of thought;
8 And by it the worlds talk one to the other; and in the Word
there were those that were silent;
9 And from it came love and concord; and they spake one to
the other whatever was theirs; and they were penetrated by
the Word;
10 And they knew Him who made them, because they were
in concord; for the mouth of the Most High spake to them;
and His explanation ran by means of it:

11 For the dwelling-place of the Word is man: and its truth is love.
12 Blessed are they who by means thereof have understood everything, and have known the Lord in His truth.
Hallelujah.

ODE 13

A strange little Ode.

1 Behold! the Lord is our mirror: open the eyes and see them in Him: and learn the manner of your face:
2 And tell forth praise to His spirit: and wipe off the filth from your face: and love His holiness and clothe yourselves therewith:
3 And be without stain at all times before Him. Hallelujah.

ODE 14

This Ode is as beautiful in style as the canonical Psalter.

1 As the eyes of a son to his father, so are my eyes, O Lord, at all times towards thee.
2 For with thee are my consolations and my delight.
3 Turn not away thy mercies from me, O Lord: and take not thy kindness from me.
4 Stretch out to me, O Lord, at all times thy right hand: and be my guide even unto the end, according to thy good pleasure.
5 Let me be well-pleasing before thee, because of thy glory and because of thy name:
6 Let me be preserved from evil, and let thy meekness, O Lord, abide with me, and the fruits of thy love.
7 Teach me the Psalms of thy truth, that I may bring forth fruit in thee:
8 And open to me the harp of thy Holy Spirit, that with all its notes I may praise thee, O Lord.
9 And according to the multitude of thy tender mercies, so thou shalt give to me; and hasten to grant our petitions; and thou art able for all our needs. Hallelujah.

ODE 15

One of the loveliest Odes in this unusual collection.

1 As the sun is the joy to them that seek for its daybreak, so is my joy the Lord;
2 Because He is my Sun and His rays have lifted me up; and His light hath dispelled all darkness from my face.
3 In Him I have acquired eyes and have seen His holy day:
4 Ears have become mine and I have heard His truth.
5 The thought of knowledge hath been mine, and I have been delighted through Him.
6 The way of error I have left, and have walked towards Him and have received salvation from Him, without grudging.
7 And according to His bounty He hath given to me, and according to His excellent beauty He hath made me.
8 I have put on incorruption through His name: and have put oft corruption by His grace.
9 Death hath been destroyed before my face: and Sheol hath been abolished by my word:
10 And there hath gone up deathless life in the Lord's land,
11 And it hath been made known to His faithful ones, and hath been given without stint to all those that trust in Him. Hallelujah.

ODE 16

The beauty of God's creation.

1 As the work of the husbandman is the ploughshare: and the work of the steersman is the guidance of the ship:
2 So also my work is the Psalm of the Lord: my craft and my occupation are in His praises:
3 Because His love bath nourished my heart, and even to my lips His fruits He poured out.
4 For my love is the Lord, and therefore I will sing unto Him:
5 For I am made strong in His praise, and I have faith in Him.
6 I will open my mouth and His spirit will utter in me the glory of the Lord and His beauty; the work of His hands and the operation of His fingers:
7 The multitude of His mercies and the strength of His word.
8 For the word of the Lord searches out all things, both the invisible and that which reveals His thought;
9 For the eye sees His works, and the ear hears His thought;
10 He spread out the earth and He settled the waters in the sea:
11 He measured the heavens and fixed the stars: and He established the creation and set it up:
12 And He rested from His works:
13 And created things run in their courses, and do their works:

14 And they know not how to stand and be idle; and His heavenly hosts are subject to His word.
15 The treasure-chamber of the light is the sun, and the treasury of the darkness is the night:
16 And He made the sun for the day that it may be bright, but night brings darkness over the face of the land;
17 And their alternations one to the other speak the beauty of God:
IS And there is nothing that is without the Lord; for He was before any thing came into being:
19 And the worlds were made by His word, and by the thought of His heart. Glory and honour to His name. Hallelujah.

ODE 17

A peculiar change of personality, scarcely realized until the return from it in the last verse.

1 I was crowned by my God: my crown is living:
2 And I was justified in my Lord: my incorruptible salvation is He.
3 I was loosed from vanity, and I was not condemned:
4 The choking bonds were cut off by her hands: I received the face and the fashion of a new person: and I walked in it and was saved;
5 And the thought of truth led me on. And I walked after it and did not wander:
6 And all that have seen me were amazed: and I was regarded by them as a strange person:
7 And He who knew and brought me up is the Most High in all His perfection. And He glorified me by His kindness, and raised my thoughts to the height of His truth.
8 And from thence He gave me the way of His precepts and I opened the doors that were closed,
9 And brake in pieces the bars of iron; but my iron melted and dissolved before me;
10 Nothing appeared closed to me: because I was the door of everything.
11 And I went over all my bondmen to loose them; that I might not leave any man bound or binding:
12 And I imparted my knowledge without grudging: and my prayer was in my love:

13 And I sowed my fruits in hearts, and transformed them
into myself: and they received my blessing and lived;
14 And they were gathered to me and were saved; because
they were to me as my own members and I was their head.
Glory to thee our head, the Lord Messiah. Hallelujah.

ODE 18

A man who had a spiritual experience brings a message.

1 My heart was lifted up in the love of the Most High and
was enlarged: that I might praise Him for His name's sake.
2 My members were strengthened that they might not fall
from His strength.
3 Sicknesses removed from my body, and it stood to the
Lord by His will. For His kingdom is true.
4 O Lord, for the sake of them that are deficient do not
remove thy word from me!
5 Neither for the sake of their works do thou restrain from
me thy perfection!
6 Let not the luminary be conquered by the darkness; nor let
truth flee away from falsehood.
7 Thou wilt appoint me to victory; our Salvation is thy right
hand. And thou wilt receive men from all quarters.
8 And thou wilt preserve whosoever is held in evils:
9 Thou art my God. Falsehood and death are not in thy
mouth:
10 For thy will is perfection; and vanity thou knowest not,
11 Nor does it know thee.
12 And error thou knowest not,
13 Neither does it know thee.
14 And ignorance appeared like a blind man; and like the
foam of the sea,
15 And they supposed of that vain thing that it was
something great;

16 And they too came in likeness of it and became vain; and
those have understood who have known and meditated;
17 And they have not been corrupt in their imagination; for
such were in the mind of the Lord;
18 And they mocked at them that were walking in error;
19 And they spake truth from the inspiration which the
Most High breathed into them; Praise and great comeliness
to His name Hallelujah.

ODE 19

Fantastic and not in harmony with the other Odes. The reference to a painless Virgin Birth is notable.

1 A cup of milk was offered to me: and I drank it in the sweetness of the delight of the Lord.
2 The Son is the cup, and He who was milked is the Father:
3 And the Holy Spirit milked Him: because His breasts were full, and it was necessary for Him that His milk should be sufficiently released;
4 And the Holy Spirit opened His bosom and mingled the milk from the two breasts of the Father; and gave the mixture to the world without their knowing:
5 And they who receive in its fulness are the ones on the right hand.
6 The Spirit opened the womb of the Virgin and she received conception and brought forth; and the Virgin became a Mother with many mercies;
7 And she travailed and brought forth a Son, without incurring pain;
8 And because she was not sufficiently prepared, and she had not sought a midwife (for He brought her to bear) she brought forth, as if she were a man, of her own will;
9 And she brought Him forth openly, and acquired Him with great dignity,
10 And loved Him in His swaddling clothes and guarded Him kindly, and showed Him in Majesty. Hallelujah.

ODE 20

A mixture of ethics and mysticism; of the golden rule and the tree of life.

1 I am a priest of the Lord, and to Him I do priestly service: and to Him I offer the sacrifice of His thought.
2 For His thought is not like the thought of the world nor the thought of the flesh, nor like them that serve carnally.
3 The sacrifice of the Lord is righteousness, and purity of heart and lips.
4 Present your reins before Him blamelessly: and let not thy heart do violence to heart, nor thy soul to soul.
5 Thou shalt not acquire a stranger by the price of thy silver, neither shalt thou seek to devour thy neighbour,
6 Neither shalt thou deprive him of the covering of his nakedness.
7 But put on the grace of the Lord without stint; and come into His Paradise and make thee a garland from its tree,
8 And put it on thy head and be glad; and recline on His rest, and glory shall go before thee,
9 And thou shalt receive of His kindness and of His grace; and thou shalt be flourishing in truth in the praise of His holiness. Praise and honour be to His name. Hallelujah.

ODE 21

A remarkable explanation of the "coats of skin" in the third chapter of Genesis.

1 My arms I lifted up to the Most High, even to the grace of
the Lord: because He had cast off my bonds from me: and
my Helper had lifted me up to His grace and to His
salvation:
2 And I put off darkness and clothed myself with light,
3 And my soul acquired a body free from sorrow or
affliction or pains.
4 And increasingly helpful to me was the thought of the
Lord, and His fellowship in incorruption:
5 And I was lifted up in His light; and I served before Him,
6 And I became near to Him, praising and confessing Him;
7 My heart ran over and was found in my mouth: and it
arose upon my lips; and the exultation of the Lord increased
on my face, and His praise likewise. Hallelujah.

ODE 22

Like the Psalms of David in their exultation because of freedom.

1 He who brought me down from on high, also brought me
up from the regions below;
2 And He who gathers together the things that are betwixt is
He also who cast me down:
3 He who scattered my enemies had existed from ancient
and my adversaries:
4 He who gave me authority over bonds that I might loose
them;
5 He that overthrew by my hands the dragon with seven
heads: and thou hast set me over his roots that I might
destroy his seed.
6 Thou wast there and didst help me, and in every place thy
name was a rampart me
7 Thy right hand destroyed his wicked poison; and thy hand
levelled the way for those who believe in thee.
8 And thou didst choose them from the graves and didst
separate them from the dead.
9 Thou didst take dead bones and didst cover them with
bodies.
10 They were motionless, and thou didst give them energy
for life.
11 Thy way was without corruption, and thy face; thou didst
bring thy world to corruption: that everything might be
dissolved, and then renewed,

12 And that the foundation for everything might be thy rock: and on it thou didst build thy kingdom; and it became the dwelling place of the saints. Hallelujah.

ODE 23

The reference to the sealed document sent by God is one of the great mysteries of the collection.

1 Joy is of the saints! and who shall put it on, but they alone?
2 Grace is of the elect! and who shall receive it except those who trust in it from the beginning?
3 Love is of the elect? And who shall put it on except those who have possessed it from the beginning?
4 Walk ye in the knowledge of the Most High without grudging: to His exultation and to the perfection of His knowledge.
5 And His thought was like a letter; His will descended from on high, and it was sent like an arrow which is violently shot from the bow:
6 And many hands rushed to the letter to seize it and to take and read it:
7 And it escaped their fingers and they were affrighted at it and at the seal that was upon it.
8 Because it was not permitted to them to loose its seal: for the power that was over the seal was greater than they.
9 But those who saw it went after the letter that they might know where it would alight, and who should read it and who should hear it.
10 But a wheel received it and came over it:
11 And there was with it a sign of the Kingdom and of the Government:

12 And everything which tried to move the wheel it mowed
and cut down:
13 And it gathered the multitude of adversaries, and
bridged the rivers and crossed over and rooted up many
forests and made a broad path.
14 The head went down to the feet, for down to the feet ran
the wheel, and that which was a sign upon it.
15 The letter was one of command, for there were included
in it all districts;
16 And there was seen at its head, the head which was
revealed even the Son of Truth from the Most High Father,
17 And He inherited and took possession of everything. And
the thought of many was brought to nought.
18 And all the apostates hasted and fled away. And those
who persecuted and were enraged became extinct.
19 And the letter was a great volume, which was wholly
written by the finger of God:
20 And the name of the Father was on it, and of the Son and
of the Holy Spirit, to rule for ever and ever. Hallelujah.

ODE 24

The mention of the Dove refers to a lost Gospel to which there are rare references in ancient writings.

1 The Dove fluttered over the Messiah, because He was her head; and she sang over Him and her voice was heard:
2 And the inhabitants were afraid and the sojourners were moved:
3 The birds dropped their wings and all creeping things died in their holes: and the abysses were opened which had been hidden; and they cried to the Lord like women in travail:
4 And no food was given to them, because it did not belong to them;
5 And they sealed up the abysses with the seal of the Lord. And they perished, in the thought, those that had existed from ancient times;
6 For they were corrupt from the beginning; and the end of their corruption was life:
7 And every one of them that was imperfect perished: for it was not possible to give them a word that they might remain:
8 And the Lord destroyed the imaginations of all them that had not the truth with them.
9 For they who in their hearts were lifted up were deficient in wisdom, and so they were rejected, because the truth was not with them.

10 For the Lord disclosed His way, and spread abroad His grace: and those who understood it, know His holiness. Hallelujah.

ODE 25

Back again to personal experience.

1 I was rescued from my bonds and unto thee, my God, I
fled:
2 For thou art the right hand of my Salvation and my helper.
3 Thou hast restrained those that rise up against me,
4 And I shall see him no more: because thy face was with
me, which saved me by thy grace.
5 But I was despised and rejected in the eye of many: and I
was in their eyes like lead,
6 And strength was mine from thyself and help.
7 Thou didst set me a lamp at my right hand and at my left:
and in me there shall be nothing that is not bright:
8 And I was clothed with the covering of thy Spirit, and thou
didst remove from me my raiment of skin;
9 For thy right hand lifted me up and removed sickness
from me:
10 And I became mighty in: the truth, and holy by thy
righteousness; and all my adversaries were afraid of me;
11 And I became admirable by the name of the Lord, and
was justified by His gentleness, and His rest is for ever and
ever. Hallelujah.

ODE 26

Remarkable praise.

1 I poured out praise to the Lord, for I am His:
2 And I will speak His holy song, for my heart is with Him.
3 For His harp is in my hands, and the Odes of His rest shall not be silent.
4 I will cry unto him from my whole heart: I will praise and exalt Him with all my members.
5 For from the east and even to the west is His praise:
6 And from the south and even to the north is the confession of Him:
7 And from the top of the hills to their utmost bound is His perfection.
8 Who can write the Psalms of the Lord, or who read them?
9 Or who can train his soul for life, that his soul may be saved,
10 Or who can rest on the Most High, so that with His mouth he may speak?
11 Who is able to interpret the wonders of the Lord?
12 For he who could interpret would be dissolved and would become that which is interpreted.
13 For it suffices to know and to rest: for in rest the singers stand,
14 Like a river which has an abundant fountain, and flows to the help of them that seek it. Hallelujah.

ODE 27

The human body makes a cross when a man stands erect in prayer with arms outstretched.

1 I stretched out my hands and sanctified my Lord:
2 For the extension of my hands is His sign:
3 And my expansion is the upright tree [or cross].

ODE 28

This Ode is a musical gem.

1 As the wings of doves over their nestlings; and the mouth of their nestlings towards their mouths.
2 So also are the wings of the Spirit over my heart:
3 My heart is delighted and exults: like the babe who exults in the womb of his mother:
4 I believed; therefore I was at rest; for faithful is He in whom I have believed:
5 He has richly blessed me and my head is with Him: and the sword shall not divide me from Him, nor the scimitar;
6 For I am ready before destruction comes; and I have been set on His immortal pinions:
7 And He showed me His sign: forth and given me to drink, and from that life is the spirit within me, and it cannot die, for it lives.
8 They who saw me marvelled at me, because I was persecuted, and they supposed that I was swallowed up: for I seemed to them as one of the lost;
9 And my oppression became my salvation; and I was their reprobation because there was no zeal in me;
10 Because I did good to every man I was hated,
11 And they came round me like mad dogs, who ignorantly attack their masters,
12 For their thought is corrupt and their understanding perverted.

13 But I was carrying water in my right hand, and their bitterness I endured by my sweetness;
14 And I did not perish, for I was not their brother nor was my birth like theirs.
15 And they sought for my death and did not find it: for I was older than the memorial of them;
16 And vainly did they make attack upon me and those who, without reward, came after me:
17 They sought to destroy the memorial of him who was before them.
18 For the thought of the Most High cannot be anticipated; and His heart is superior to all wisdom. Hallelujah.

ODE 29

Again reminiscent of the Psalms, of David.

1 The Lord is my hope: in Him I shall not be confounded.
2 For according to His praise He made me, and according to
His goodness even so He gave unto me:
3 And according to His mercies He exalted me: and
according to His excellent beauty He set me on high:
4 And brought me up out of the depths of Sheol: and from
the mouth of death He drew me:
5 And thou didst lay my enemies low, and He justified me
by His grace.
6 For I believed in the Lord's Messiah: and it appeared to me
that He is the Lord;
7 And He showed him His sign: and He led me by His light,
and gave me the rod of His power;
8 That I might subdue the imaginations of the peoples; and
the power of the men of might to bring them low:
9 To make war by His word, and to take victory by His
power.
10 And the Lord overthrew my enemy by His word: and he
became like the stubble which the wind carries away;
11 And I gave praise to the Most High because He exalted
me His servant and the son of His handmaid. Hallelujah.

ODE 30

An invitation to the thirsty.

1 Fill ye waters for yourselves from the living fountain of the
Lord, for it is opened to you:
2 And come all ye thirsty, and take the draught; and rest by
the fountain of the Lord.
3 For fair it is and pure and gives rest to the soul. Much
more pleasant are its waters than honey;
4 And the honeycomb of bees is not to be compared with it.
5 For it flows forth from the lips of the Lord and from the
heart of the Lord is its name.
6 And it came infinitely and invisibly: and until it was set in
the midst they did not know it:
7 Blessed are they who have drunk therefrom and have
found rest thereby. Hallelujah.

ODE 31

A song that Marcus Aurelius might have known when he said "Be like the promontory against which the waves continually break."

1 The abysses were dissolved before the Lord: and darkness was destroyed by His appearance:
2 Error went astray and perished at His hand: and folly found no path to walk in, and was submerged by the truth of the Lord.
3 He opened His mouth and spake grace and joy: and He spake a new song of praise to His name:
4 And He lifted up His voice to the Most High, and offered to Him the sons that were with Him.
5 And His face was justified, for thus His holy Father had given to Him.
6 Come forth, ye that have been afflicted and receive joy, and possess your souls by His grace; and take to you immortal life.
7 And they made me a debtor when I rose up, me who had been a debtor: and they divided my spoil, though nothing was due to them.
8 But I endured and held my peace and was silent, as if not, moved by them.
9 But I stood unshaken like a firm rock which is beaten by the waves and endures.
10 And I bore their bitterness for humility's sake:
11 In order, that I might redeem my people, and inherit it

and that I might not make void my promises to the fathers, to whom I promised the salvation of their seed. Hallelujah.

ODE 32

Joy and light.

1 To the blessed there is joy from their hearts, and light from Him that dwells in them:
2 And words from the Truth, who was self-originate: for He is strengthened by the holy power of the Most High: and He is unperturbed for ever and ever. Hallelujah.

ODE 33

A virgin stands and proclaims (v. 5).

1 Again Grace ran and forsook corruption, and came down in Him to bring it to nought;
2 And He destroyed perdition from before Him, and devastated all its order;
3 And He stood on a lofty summit and uttered His voice from one end of the earth to the other:
4 And drew to Him all those who obeyed Him; and there did not appear as it were an evil person.
5 But there stood a perfect virgin who was proclaiming and calling and saying,
6 O ye sons of men, return ye, and ye daughters of men, come ye:
7 And forsake the ways of that corruption and draw near unto me, and I will enter into you, and will bring you forth from perdition,
8 And make you wise in the ways of truth: that you be not destroyed nor perish:
9 Hear ye me and be redeemed. For the grace of God I am telling among you: and by my means you shall be redeemed and become blessed.
10 I am your judge; and they who have put me on shall not be injured: but they shall possess the new world that is incorrupt:

11 My chosen ones walk in me, and my ways I will make known to them that seek me, and I will make them trust in my name. Hallelujah.

ODE 34

True poetry--pure and simple.

1 No way is hard where there is a simple heart.
2 Nor is there any wound where the thoughts are upright:
3 Nor is there any storm in the depth of the illuminated thought:
4 Where one is surrounded on every side by beauty, there is nothing that is divided.
5 The likeness of what is below is that which is above; for everything is above: what is below is nothing but the imagination of those that are without knowledge.
6 Grace has been revealed for your salvation. Believe and live and be saved. Hallelujah.

ODE 35

"No cradled child more softly lies than I: come soon, eternity."

1 The dew of the Lord in quietness He distilled upon me:
2 And the cloud of peace He caused to rise over my head,
which guarded me continually;
3 It was to me for salvation: everything was shaken and they
were affrighted;
4 And there came forth from them a smoke and a judgment;
and I was keeping quiet in the order of the Lord:
5 More than shelter was He to me, and more than
foundation.
6 And I was carried like a child by his mother: and He gave
me milk, the dew of the Lord:
7 And I grew great by His bounty, and rested in His
perfection,
8 And I spread out my hands in the lifting up of my soul:
and I was made right with the Most High, and I was
redeemed with Him. Hallelujah.

ODE 36

Theologians have never agreed on an explanation of this perplexing Ode.

1 I rested in the Spirit of the Lord: and the Spirit raised me on high:
2 And made me stand on my feet in the height of the Lord, before His perfection and His glory, while I was praising Him by the composition of His songs.
3 The Spirit brought me forth before the face of the Lord: and, although a son of man, I was named the Illuminate, the Son of God:
4 While I praised amongst the praising ones, and great was I amongst the mighty ones.
5 For according to the greatness of the Most High, so He made me: and like His own newness He renewed me; and He anointed me from His own perfection:
6 And I became one of His Neighbours; and my mouth was opened, like a cloud of dew,
7 And my heart poured out as it were a gushing stream of righteousness,
8 And my access to Him was in peace; and I was established by the Spirit of His government. Hallelujah.

ODE 37

An elementary Ode.

1 I stretched out my hands to my Lord: and to the Most I
High I raised my voice:
2 And I spake with the lips of my heart; and He heard me,
when my voice reached I Him:
3 His answer came to me, and gave me the fruits of my
labours;
4 And it gave me rest by the grace of the Lord. Hallelujah.

ODE 38

A beautiful description of the power of truth.

1 I went up to the light of truth as if into a chariot:
2 And the Truth took me and led me: and carried me across pits and gulleys; and from the rocks and the waves it preserved me:
3 And it became to me a haven of Salvation: and set me on the arms of immortal life:
4 And it went with me and made me rest, and suffered me not to wander, because it was the Truth;
5 And I ran no risk, because I walked with Him;
6 And I did not make an error in anything because I obeyed the Truth.
7 For Error flees away from it, and meets it not: but the Truth proceeds in the right path, and
8 Whatever I did not know, it made clear to me, all the poisons of error, and the plagues of death which they think to be sweetness:
9 And I saw the destroyer of destruction, when the bride who is corrupted is adorned: and the bridegroom who corrupts and is corrupted;
10 And I asked the Truth 'Who are these?'; and He said to me, 'This is the deceiver and the error:
11 And they are alike in the beloved and in his bride: and they lead astray and corrupt the whole world:
12 And they invite many to the banquet,

13 And give them to drink of the wine of their intoxication,
and remove their wisdom and knowledge, and so they make
them without intelligence;
14 And then they leave them; and then these go about like
madmen corrupting: seeing that-they are without heart, nor
do they seek for it!
15 And I was made wise so as not to fall into the hands of
the deceiver; and I congratulated myself because the Truth
went with me,
16 And I was established and lived and was redeemed,
17 And my foundations were laid on the hand of the Lord:
because He established me.
18 For He set the root and watered it and fixed it and blessed
it; and its fruits are for ever.
19 It struck deep and sprung up and spread out, and was
full and enlarged;
20 And the Lord alone was glorified in His planting and in
His husbandry: by His care and by the blessing of His lips,
21 By the beautiful planting of His right hand: and by the
discovery of His planting, and by the thought of His mind.
Hallelujah.

ODE 39

One of the few allusions to events in the Gospels--that of our Lord walking on the Sea of Galilee.

1 Great rivers are the power of the Lord:
2 And they carry headlong those who despise Him: and entangle their paths:
3 And they sweep away their fords, and catch their bodies and destroy their lives.
4 For they are more swift than lightning and more rapid, and those who cross them in faith are not moved;
5 And those who walk on them without blemish shall not be afraid.
6 For the sign in them is the Lord; and the sign is the way of those who cross in the name of the Lord;
7 Put on, therefore, the name of the Most High, and know Him, and you shall cross without danger, for the rivers will be subject to you.
8 The Lord has bridged them by His word; and He walked and crossed them on foot:
9 And His footsteps stand firm on the water, and are not injured; they are as firm as a tree that is truly set up.
10 And the waves were lifted up on this side and on that, but the footsteps of our Lord Messiah stand firm and are not obliterated and are not defaced.
11 And a way has been appointed for those who cross after Him and for those who adhere to the course of faith in Him and worship His name. Hallelujah.

ODE 40

A song of praise without equal.

1 As the honey distills from the comb of the bees,
2 And the milk flows from the woman that loves her children;
3 So also is my hope on Thee, my God.
4 As the fountain gushes out its water,
5 So my heart gushes out the praise of the Lord and my lips utter praise to Him, and my tongue His psalms.
6 And my face exults with His gladness, and my spirit exults in His love, and my soul shines in Him:
7 And reverence confides in Him; and redemption in Him stands assured:
8 And His inheritance is immortal life, and those who participate in it are incorrupt. Hallelujah.

ODE 41

We discover that the writer may be a Gentile (v. 8).

1 All the Lord's children will praise Him, and will collect the truth of His faith.
2 And His children shall be known to Him. Therefore we will sing in His love:
3 We live in the Lord by His grace: and life we receive in His Messiah:
4 For a great day has shined upon us: and marvellous is He who has given us of His glory.
5 Let us, therefore, all of us unite together in the name of the Lord, and let us honour Him in His goodness,
6 And let our faces shine in His light: and let our hearts meditate in His love by night and by day.
7 Let us exult with the joy of the Lord.
8 All those will be astonished that see me. For from another race am I:
9 For the Father of truth remembered me: He who possessed me from the beginning:
10 For His bounty begat me, and the thought of His heart:
11 And His Word is with us in all our way;
12 The Saviour who makes alive and does not reject our souls-;
13 The man who was humbled, and exalted by His own righteousness,
14 The Son of the Most High appeared in the perfection of His Father;

15 And light dawned from the Word that was beforetime in
Him;
16 The Messiah is truly one; and He was known before the
foundation of the world,
17 That He might save souls for ever by the truth of His
name: a new song arises from those who love Him.
Hallelujah.

ODE 42

The Odes of Solomon, the Son of David, are ended with the following exquisite verses.

1 I stretched out my hands and approached my Lord:
2 For the stretching of my hands is His sign:
3 My expansion is the outspread tree which was set up on the way of the Righteous One.
4 And I became of no account to those who did not take hold of me; and I shall be with those who love me.
5 All my persecutors are dead; and they sought after me who hoped in me, because I was alive:
6 And I rose up and am with them; and I will speak by their mouths.
7 For they have despised those who persecuted them;
8 And I lifted up over them the yoke of my love;
9 Like the arm of the bridegroom over the bride,
10 So was my yoke over those that know me:
11 And as the couch that is spread in the house of the bridegroom and bride,
12 So is my love over those that believe in me.
13 And I was not rejected though I was reckoned to be so.
14 I did not perish, though they devised it against me.
15 Sheol saw me and was made miserable:
16 Death cast me up, and many along with me.
17 I had gall and bitterness, and I went down with him to the utmost of his depth:

18 And the feet and the head he let go, for they were not able
to endure my face:
19 And I made a congregation of living men amongst his
dead men, and I spake with them by living lips:
20 Because my word shall not be void:
21 And those who had died ran towards me: and they cried
and said, Son of God, have pity on us, and do with us
according to thy kindness,
22 And bring us out from the bonds of darkness: and open
to us the door by which we shall come out to thee.
23 For we see that our death has not touched thee.
24 Let us also be redeemed with thee: for thou art our
Redeemer.
25 And I heard their voice; and my name I sealed upon their
heads:
26 For they are free men and they are mine. Hallelujah.

ABELA BOOKS IN THE LOST BOOKS OF EDEN SERIES

The First and Second Books of Adam and Eve
The Book of the Secrets of Enoch
The Psalms of Solomon and the Odes of Solomon
The Letter of Aristeas
The Fourth Book of Maccabees,
The Story of Ahikar
The Testaments of the Twelve Patriarchs
- The Testament of Reuben
- The Testament of Simeon
- The Testament of Levi
- The Testament of Judah
- The Testament of Issachar
- The Testament of Zebulun
- The Testament of Dan
- The Testament of Naphtali
- The Testament Of Gad
- The Testament of Asher
- The Testament of Joseph
- The Testament of Benjamin

Lightning Source UK Ltd.
Milton Keynes UK
UKHW040153061218
333501UK00001B/59/P

9 781909 302303